CHILD-1

EARLY WRITING

Ideas for engaging young children in the early writing process

LYNN CLERE & BRIDIE RABAN

ts

TEACHING
SOLUTIONS

Acknowledgements

Valuable feedback has been received from the educators and children at Mildura West Kindergarten and Pasadena Preschool & Country Way Early Learning (Mildura).

Published in 2017 by TEACHING SOLUTIONS
PO Box 197
Albert Park 3206
Australia

info@teachingsolutions.com.au
www.teachingsolutions.com.au

Cover design: Tom Kurema
Photographs: Sam Goodman, istock, Fotolia
Printed in Australia by OPUS Group

09-2017

Contents

Introduction

We wonder if you picked up this book initially because the title grabbed you. We wonder if you smiled at the idea of child-initiated early writing. All of us can think of several children who would rather, and indeed do, run a mile rather than write. Does the idea of these children coming willingly to a writing activity seem unlikely?

The ideas in this book will need support and guidance initially, as children come to learn about writing. As with most, if not all, early years activities, children have to be shown how to use the resources first. But it will not be long before they are not only able to manage the activity by themselves but adapt and extend it, as well as clear away afterwards. Wherever possible and appropriate, have resources readily accessible so that children can set up activities themselves with minimal support and thus make their mark-making and 'writing' truly child-initiated.

Learning to write takes many years, patience and much perseverance. This book is about finding lots of different ways to make that long process fun and productive for both the child and educator during the years before formal schooling begins.

Case studies that demonstrate how using this holistic approach facilitates learning across more than one area are included where relevant. While learning about writing, our children can also be learning about other important aspects of their world.

With the pressure of government targets, literacy levels and NAPLAN, we tend to make heavy weather of learning to write. Teaching a child to be a fluent writer is going to take several school years, so why not spend time pleasurably and purposefully in the years before school while the children are learning about writing?

Children need to see that even the educators in their setting can enjoy doodling and taking pleasure in the colour and texture of different media without feeling defined by the outcomes. The process of writing should be enjoyable and exciting but can be thwarted if there is the undue pressure of a desired outcome.

Sometimes we need to remind ourselves that we are human 'beings' not only human 'becomings'. We need to enable the children in our care to simply 'be' – enjoying where they are at and not worrying about and planning for the next steps and what they will become. As Carlina Rinaldi says:

> We don't talk about preparing children for the future; it is the present that is important. We do not know what the future holds. Childhood is the best time of life, it should be enjoyed.

We are all writers, even if the writing that we produce does not resemble the work of an award-winning author. Our writing should be enjoyed and celebrated.

Our children also need to experience 'non-writing' writing. Writing does not have to happen in formal, sitting down with paper and pencil situations. There are many exciting multisensory media in which we can 'write'; for example, writing in paste is very therapeutic for a hot and bothered educator as well as their hot and bothered children. Writing does not have to be and, indeed, should not always be permanent. Many children want to be able to wipe away their mark-making or watch it evaporate in front of their very eyes.

As their writing disappears so do any imperfections, and many children welcome that.

Disappearing writing takes on a magical quality as does 'magic writing' (see p. 11) with resistance materials such as wax crayons and paint. Making writing magical can only entice children to want to write more.

Some educators may be concerned about the mess involved in these activities and also that resources might be wasted. We cannot say that these are not messy activities, as many of them are, but we have successfully done most of these activities indoors with well-protected floors, spillable pots placed in larger trays and with minimum supervision. Most also lend themselves well to being outdoor activities.

We have to learn to observe from a distance, supporting the children's autonomy to have a go at mixing their own paints, for instance, and learning from their own mistakes. Putting smaller amounts of paint powder into smaller tubs helps, and the children can handle these easily. Small yogurt pots can be used for paint powder and empty liquid soap dispensers are perfect for adding water.

A large picture instruction poster on the wall showing the amount of powder to water required and the basics of colour mixing enables the children to take control. Then leave them to experiment, only helping out if asked or if absolutely necessary. Give lots of praise.

For the first week this will be more time consuming than merely mixing the paint yourself but gradually the effort will be well worth it. As the children learn how to do the task, you will notice their language use and interactions increasing and becoming more complex. They will learn about how materials change according to the amount of water added, and how colours can be mixed, and they will generally become more active learners.

Some educators may be reluctant to introduce such child-led learning. We are changing long held views on what is effective practice but in doing so we are working towards best practice where our children are active learners and confident about initiating their own learning. In order to do this, we must empower them to access the resources in our settings.

Equally, we must empower all our colleagues to let the children have a go and not worry when mistakes and spills occur. Children learn as much, if not more, from their mistakes. They should be helped to regard spills and errors as merely part of the learning process in a relaxed and happy setting and not anything to be concerned about. If we make a mess, we clean it up – no problem.

Children learning about writing, or indeed learning about anything, in a relaxed and happy environment will learn more quickly and be better able to build on that early learning later on.

In order to facilitate a learning environment that best supports child initiated writing, a list of key questions is included at the end of each chapter for educators to consider as a team. This list features questions to promote discussion and to be used as a basis for future planning.

Early writing development

A useful overview of children's early writing development is provided in the following tables. Each table looks at early writing development from four different perspectives:

- Composition
- Written language
- Concepts about print
- Handwriting

Table 1 gives ideas for the educator to think about against each of these four perspectives.

Writing is a complex activity made up of a variety of aspects which progress at different rates depending on purpose and opportunity. A helpful progression that young children move through is outlined in table 2, which outlines the trajectories that children may take as their understanding of the purpose and functions of writing develops.

Table 1. *Supporting early writing development in the preschool years*

Writing components	Suggested activities (for educators)
Writing as composition	• Look at writing in the community or around the room and talk about this. How is information conveyed and why? • Children will use drawings to convey their ideas. Have children 'read' their drawings which can then be scribed for them. • 'What will we draw today?' encourages children to think about their own stories or pieces of information to 'write' about with adult scribing.
Written language v. spoken language	• Story-telling helps children to focus on the language. • Encourage and support children to say more for you to scribe to their drawing. • Opportunities to talk about things in the past or future require the language to be more detailed and explicit. • 'Pretending' not to understand what a child says can provide opportunities for explanations and requests with more explicit language.
Concepts about print	• Point to individual words as you read what is scribed • Help child to understand that it's the squiggles on the page that tell the story, not the picture. • Give them the idea of directionality, top of page, moving left to right, by following the text with your finger. • Show and respond to exclamation marks. • Make two name cards for each child to match from a mixed set.
Handwriting	• Play games developing large muscle movements from the shoulder, such as throwing a ball into a container. • Provide music for children to make arm movements. • Add pincers and tweezers to a tray of buttons or marbles for sorting. • Have a writing table with pots of different pens, pencils, textas and crayons. • Add different sizes of coloured paper for pattern-making, e.g. /\/\/\/\/\/\/\ OOOOOOOOOOO

Table 2. *Early writing development in the preschool years*

Writing components	Suggested progression
Writing as composition	• Children make marks to stand for objects and ideas. • Children use drawings to convey their ideas and stories. • Children 'read' their drawings and what has been scribed for them.

Written language v. spoken language	• Scribing to drawing, the child uses increasingly complex language, e.g.
	  ◦ 'That's my dog.'
	  ◦ 'This is my dog and he has long fluffy hair.'
	  ◦ 'My dog has long fluffy hair and he likes to go for walks.'
	  ◦ 'My dog loves his bones but sometimes he buries them in the yard and Dad gets really cross.'

Concepts about print	• Children make random squiggles that do not resemble letters. • Children write some letter-like forms, usually letters from their own name, some upside down and backwards. • Children work across the page from left to right. • Children leave spaces between marks and letters.
Handwriting	• Large muscle movements from the shoulder, for instance, throwing a large ball then a small one. • Using arm and elbow movements in time to music. • Using finger movements to pick up and sort buttons or marbles. • Using textas to make marks on paper • Using pincers or tweezers to play a game, eg. moving small objects round a board. • Using pens and pencils to make patterns on paper. • Copying name activities.

1. Writing using multisensory media

'Children ... engage in increasingly complex sensory-motor skills and movement patterns. [They] combine gross and fine motor movement and balance to achieve increasingly complex patterns of activity ... [and] use their sensory capabilities and dispositions with increasing integration, skill and purpose to explore and respond to their world' (EYLF p. 32).

Writing in the early years is of course synonymous with mark-making and finger painting. 'Writing' covers all aspects of mark-making, and finger painting is really finger writing. Finger painting is the first step in mark-making.

We often see babies 'writing' in food spillages on their high chair table and looking quite surprised and pleased with themselves as they see the results of their efforts. Meal times can then become an even more protracted affair.

Finger writing can be enjoyed by very young children who find it difficult to hold a writing implement and by older children who enjoy the freedom from having to control a pen, pencil or brush. It helps to build finger strength and enhances fine motor skills but also offers an additional dimension – for many children nothing can be more exciting than the deliciously tactile experience of paint or shaving foam, for instance, squelching through their fingers.

For this reason, expect little distinguishable mark-making on the first few occasions, as many children will initially explore the medium before actually using it to make any specific marks.

Over the years we have learnt that some children are frightened of making mistakes – sad but true. Writing in these kinds of media can easily be erased by the writer if they are not pleased with the result. This can build confidence in these children to simply 'have a go', and when you feel that the time is right you can gently praise their efforts. 'What a shame you rubbed that out, I thought it was brilliant/so clever, etc. I wonder if you could write it again to show your friends? I bet they'll love it too.'

Comments casually made with no pressure, as you are gently pottering in the same medium or seemingly busy doing something else, can spur a child on to further 'work' and progress with no hint of correcting their work or any judgement having been made. We can all thrive in a relaxed learning environment.

The media described in this chapter are often messy and will need to be contained. You might want children to wear aprons, which

Shaving foam

Add a light spray of shaving foam to the tray. Shaving foam has more 'wow' factor than shaving gel as the foam tends to float in wisps. Encourage the children to draw in the foam – smiley faces, houses, pets, favourite toys, etc. Can they write the first letter of their name? You can encourage this in a relaxed atmosphere by simply drawing your own pet, writing your own name in the foam and saying what you are doing. Most children will do similarly, not just to please you but to prove that they can do it too!

Expect a lot of excited squeals with this activity and aprons are a must!

Case study

should be roomy and easy for them to put on themselves, with some help from a friend, to encourage independence.

Suitable containers would be a water tray, sand tray, or builder's tray but these can be expensive and are often already being used for another activity. Baking trays offer a cheap alternative as do brightly coloured cat litter trays (brand new and unused of course). New cat litter trays fit neatly on a table, can accommodate one or two children's activity and are light and safe enough for children to handle, carry and clean up when setting up or tidying away.

Jack rarely spoke to the children or educators in his group. When he first started at the setting he had spoken but the children found it difficult to understand him. No one had been unkind to him, but Jack had been embarrassed. He seemed to resign himself to the fact that it was easier to say little or nothing at all and rely on gesture and body language than to try to enter into further verbal communication.

The educators at the setting became more and more concerned that Jack was engaging in behaviours similar to those of an elective mute. One morning the educator asked Jack to help her to set up a writing activity.

'What would you like to write with today?' she asked pointing to the various packs of textas, paints, shaving foam, etc. on the shelf.

Jack picked up the shaving foam and pointed to the writing trays for her to carry to the writing table with him.

'I wonder if anyone else would like to join in with us?' she asked in a slightly louder tone, knowing that she would have several volunteers offering to join her and the shaving foam.

Jack smiled at the other children and joined in as they all helped each other into their aprons. 'Thanks Jack,' said Ben giving a thumbs-up sign. Jack returned the thumbs-up and grinned.

The children started by just feeling the foam. 'Oooh it's all soft and lovely.' 'It's bubbly.' 'My Dad's got this stuff at home, he does this,' and Lucy put the foam on her chin. The children shrieked with laughter, looking towards the educator to see if this was acceptable. The educator smiled and said that Lucy looked like Father Christmas. The children found this highly amusing and several of them also put the foam on their chins. In their excitement wisps of the foam were floating about them.

With everyone's attention diverted by the wisps and the excitement enveloping the Father Christmases perhaps Jack's perceived pressure to talk, and to be seen to be talking, lifted somewhat. Anyway, he started chattering away maybe to himself, maybe to the other children.

'Bubbles, bubbles,' he repeated as he scooped up the foam in his hands and threw it in the air. 'Look, Jack is talking!' gasped one of the children. 'Of course', said the educator as nonchalantly as she could, smiling. 'Course!' said Jack busily, not even looking up.

We have done the same activity with very young children who have little language but who, while doing the activity, have made gurgles, sounds and exclamations of pleasure. Reaffirming these sounds, commenting on their mark-making progress, without any pressure of expectation of a reply, is probably the best course of action by the educator. A reciprocal, if non-verbal, language exchange can be an enjoyable communication experience and meanwhile the children can build their fine motor skills and develop their language as well as an awareness of writing.

Activities such as shaving foam offer such a 'wow' factor and the children become so absorbed in what they are doing that they can overcome barriers such as speech and social interaction difficulties, which may have seemed impossible. Holistic multisensory experiences really do offer opportunities to cover several EYLF learning outcomes at the same time.

Of course some children do not enjoy messy activities and this should be accepted and understood. This is discussed further alongside the case study about Sam in chapter 2.

Sand

Add sand – coloured or plain – to the tray. This can provide a quieter writing experience than that offered by the larger room sand tray. Other media can be mixed in such as coloured glitter to make it more exciting.

Traditional finger painting

Finger painting is easy and uncomplicated, and offers opportunities for children to learn more about colour mixing. When the children help you to mix the paint colours, limit the palette to the primary colours and suggest they try to make more colours themselves from the red, yellow and blue. Use a thick consistency of paint and either 'paint' in the tray or on art paper or rolls of wrapping paper. Add sand or glitter to the paint to get additional texture.

'Magic writing' – resistance writing inspires resistant writers

Use a resistance media (white wax crayon or a white pastel stick) to write a message, a child's name, a smiley face, etc. on white art paper. Encourage children to mix their own colour palette to colour wash the paper in their favourite colours – the resistance material does not take up the colour wash and the message/name is thus revealed. Young children find this very exciting – be prepared to have to do this many many times.

These tactile media can also be used to explore pattern, shape, size and position.

Writing on laminated pages

Laminated pages will have a limited life span and will need replacing every few months. However, in the meantime occasional cleaning with a whiteboard cleaner will extend their life and make them more inviting to use. It's a good idea to rotate their use anyway, ensuring that you remove less popular pages and regularly offer new pages to maintain interest.

File less popular pages away as what may not appeal to one group of children can be an instant success with another group. You can include a new page or two every Monday. The children soon got used to this and used to immediately go to see what was new for them to write on. Gradually they even began to bring in their own pages to be laminated for them.

Window writing

Window writing using whiteboard marker pens is also exciting as it offers the 'wow' factor of an activity not usually experienced at home. Children need to be advised that this activity might not be possible or appropriate at home. Remember to test a small inconspicuous space first to make sure that you can clean the marker pen off completely.

If window writing is a success then you can buy window pens, which last longer. These will offer a more permanent display but will need a specific cleaning agent recommended by the pen manufacturer. Again, check on an inconspicuous area of window that they can be removed eventually.

Wipe-away writing

Some children are more comfortable with their writing if they can instantly wipe away what they are not proud of – so wipe-away writing can have an important place in children's learning about writing. Other children love the 'magic' aspect of writing that can just disappear with the wipe of a hand.

Provide whiteboards – individual and wall mounted – and maker pens with erasers and cloths for wiping away. (See also 'writing on laminated pages' on p. 11)

Outdoor water painting

It is the temporary aspect of this writing that makes 'painting' outdoors with water so popular. Mark-making with water cannot be seen so clearly and so any 'mistakes' the writer feels he or she may have made will soon evaporate anyway.

Water painting also appeals to children who enjoy making large movements in their writing and do not like to be confined to a piece of paper. Water is not as messy as paint either, so some children who may feel a little clumsy with paint spills may be more at ease with outdoor water painting.

On rainy days water won't be needed as the children can 'write' on the wet windows.

Key questions

Writing using multisensory media can easily be incorporated into your daily planning rather than kept as special one-off activities. The following questions may help you and your colleagues to think about the best way of incorporating multisensory media resources into each day's writing activities.

☐ Are all educators happy and relaxed about mess and its contribution to learning about writing?

☐ Do we have a shared understanding of how tactile media will contribute to our children's writing progress?

☐ Have we taken time to experience the different media ourselves, discussing creative and non-creative mess?

☐ Do all educators and families value tactile media? Do we need to consider further training?

☐ Are aprons readily available at child height and can the children put these on independently or with the help of a friend?

☐ Are resources set out so that children can readily manage their own mess? Are cleaning materials readily and safely available? Have the children been shown how to tidy up after themselves and are they encouraged to do this after every session ready for the next person to use?

☐ Are any children nervous about getting messy or dirty? Will any of them need additional support or collaborative adult play until they feel more comfortable about joining in?

☐ Do any children have known allergies? Do we have a supply of non-allergenic gloves readily available? Have we discussed their use with relevant family members of children with known allergies and do we have a list of suitable alternative activities for these children?

☐ Do we consider it necessary to obtain parental permission for use of some of these media?

Notes

_____
_____
_____
_____
_____
_____
_____
_____
_____
_____
_____
_____
_____
_____
_____
_____
_____
_____
_____
_____
_____
_____
_____

Links with the EYLF learning outcomes

Make a note of any evidence for the following elements you may observe:

1. Strong sense of identity
- Confidently explores and engages with new activities
- Initiates and also joins in activities
- Persists when faced with challenges

2. Connected with and contributes to their world
- Responds in a variety of ways to what they see, hear, smell, touch and feel
- Listens to the ideas of others and respects different ways of being and doing
- Participates with others to solve problems and contributes to group outcomes

3. A strong sense of wellbeing
- Continues to be interested, excited and motivated to learn
- Recognises the contribution they make to shared projects and experiences
- Engages in increasingly complex sensory-motor skills and movement patterns

4. Confident and involved learner
- Is a curious and confident participant
- Engages with and co-constructs learning
- Experiences the benefits and pleasures of shared learning environments

5. Effective communicator
- Begins to use images and approximations of letters and words to convey meanings
- Experiments with ways of expressing ideas and meaning using a range of media
- Uses symbols to represent and make meaning.

2. Writing without pens or pencils

'Children learn that drawing is different from making accidental marks. They start to explore a range of media and implements and see what can be done with them' (Palmer, Bayley & Raban 2014, p. 92).

Chapter 1 looked at mark-making and writing using multisensory media. The best practice for the early years learning opportunities naturally involves a multisensory holistic approach. The activities covered in chapter 1 will appeal to young children and offer the 'wow' factor. They are also fairly messy and will require some supervision, at least until the children have understood how to handle the media and your expectations!

The activities in this chapter still offer multisensory approaches, but with slightly less messy materials. If your team of educators is nervous about messy activities or believes productive writing can only be formed with pens and pencils, then the activities in this chapter could be a good starting point.

The activities here are still a little bit different. They involve fun tactile activities that are less messy but children will still be learning important things about writing.

Writing with string and wool

In our settings we all have craft materials which lend themselves well to letter formation. Indeed, while working on collage with wool, string and threads, children sometimes notice

that the length of fibre has fallen into a shape resembling a letter in their name and point this out.

Engagement with these materials had aspects of our fibre collage play, but was also a different tactile media for the children to experience. So a different media choice was moving learning on. It is also a wonderful messy activity, particularly if you add water or paints.

As mentioned in chapter 1, you need to be aware that some children dislike messy activities – sometimes to the point of phobia. These children should never be coerced, cajoled or coaxed into messy activities. However, they should see what is happening and how the other children are enjoying what they are doing. That way they can come to see messy activity for what it is – lots of fun and totally non-threatening. They should also learn that while there are some rules that must be kept to ensure a safe and happy environment, we all have choices and our likes/dislikes and feelings generally will never be dismissed or ignored.

We like children to experience as many of the activities as possible as we then feel that they have indeed enjoyed 'broad and balanced' opportunities. But children can experience the activity by simply observing, which is what many do with particular types of activity that they are unfamiliar with or uncertain of.

In the following case study we, as educators, didn't considered the activity to be particularly messy. We had experienced far worse in previous sessions. But for Sam this was most definitely messy to the point of causing him distress.

Case study

Sam disliked messy activities. He hated having dirty hands, whether the dirt was sand, paint, glue or even food. He became extremely upset and had to wash his hands immediately. His distress was painful to see and temper tantrums followed very quickly if he wasn't able to wash immediately.

One day his educator was working with the children with a tray of woollen threads in water. First of all we 'squished and squashed' our hands through the mixture. Shrieks of 'It's all swishy' and 'Look mine's like a worm!' drew a lot of attention from the other children.

Sam was no exception. He stopped playing with the cars and garage (a safe game as he perceived this to be entirely free from any chance of getting dirty) and stood up to watch. Some of the other children were invited to join in but the invitation was deliberately not extended to Sam. Gradually he came forward, and after about ten minutes was standing next to the educator.

By this time the children had decided that the swirling wool lengths in water was indeed a tray of worms and had started to lay strands of wool along side each other to work out whose was the longest. Some mathematical language was introduced – long, longer, longest, short, shorter, shortest. Sam enjoyed maths and became even more interested in the activity. As 'worms' were compared, the educator began to label hers as 'Sam's and my worm'. Sam smiled.

'What colour would you like the worms to be, Sam?' his educator asked. 'Green', he whispered. So Sam had the task of finding the wool colour of his choice and the rest of the group joined in. The educator took one worm out of the trough and began to sing, 'There's a worm at the bottom of the yard' and some children joined in, while others continued to work with the swirling wool in the tray. On the palm of her hand, the educator arranged the wet piece of wool into an 'S' and said to Sam – 'Look now the worm is in the shape of the first letter in your name.'

A few seconds later Sam was working with the wet and colour-dyed wool, albeit just one strand but for him this was progress. Any horror at dirty hands was prompted by suggesting we all washed our hands together because our hands were now a little green and we would make everything we touched green. Some adventurous children touched their faces and ran to the mirror squealing with glee at their green reflections.

Later in the morning, Sam led me to the wool and water tray and together we completed some 'worm writing'.

Over the next few months Sam began to enjoy some messy activities. By the time he left to start school his phobia had eased somewhat; his distress subsided and tantrums were a thing of the past. He voluntarily engaged in many aspects of messy activity knowing that he could withdraw at any time and he could always wash his hands whenever he wished.

Sam is never likely in the near future to put messy activity at the very top of his favourite activities but he did enjoy some messy activity and he no longer felt the huge upset that he had originally suffered from.

While this had been an opportunity to engage reluctant writers with messy activities, in fact a reluctant child had been engaged in messy activities by using his interest in maths and letters.

Moulds, templates and stencils

Filling alphabet moulds with sand or coloured, bubbled or scented water will help to strengthen hands and fingers, thus improving fine motor skills. This activity is pleasingly tactile and can help those children who find the actual physical process of writing difficult.

Activities that include such experiential opportunities can also help those children with speech and communication problems. This writing 'picture' is surrounded by letter stamps 'A' and 'B'.

Collage writing

Children who are interested in writing and the written word, the finished product and its purpose, may not yet be ready to actually write for themselves. Similarly, while many children are not bothered whether or not their

writing resembles an adult's writing or that found in a storybook, others are acutely aware that their writing is not readily understood and grow tired of translating it. It is usually well-meaning adults who ask for translation, whereas children are often very accepting of their peer's hieroglyphic marks.

It would therefore seem reasonable to provide opportunities to write which do not necessarily require pen, paper and the ability to form recognisable letters. Collage writing fulfils this requirement. Children can use printed fonts and scripts, cutting and sticking the letters to form words, or use other materials to form their own letters. Either way a writing collage is formed.

Resources ideas for collage writing

- A variety of different papers – printer paper, coloured paper, envelopes, off-cuts of card etc.

- A selection of printed scripts in a variety of fonts – these can be printed from the computer, or be from magazine and newspaper pages. Try to offer print that is both upper and lower case and in a variety of colours, as children notice and will comment on differences and similarities. This can offer opportunities for discussion of fonts and consolidation of colour knowledge. After cutting out letters from magazines in the home corner, Dave 'wrote' his name.

- Other media can be used to form letters rather than actual letters themselves, e.g. coloured mosaic paper squares, string, wool, thread, sand, glitter.
- Stickers

- Glue
  - White liquid glue – messy but fun! Very young children will play with the glue initially rather than actually use it for their sticking project. Let them play with the glue – they are learning what makes glue, glue: what its properties are and what it can do. Without this initial exploration, a vital piece of learning has been missed.
  - Glue stick – not so messy and very easy for young children to use independently.

Note: Please let children help you to mix paints and glue. It's a much slower process, of course, but they will learn about how materials (in this case paint powder) can be changed by adding water.

As we work with young children we need to be aware of all the learning opportunities there are throughout the day, even in the preparation of our resources. The children will have ownership of their work if they have chosen what to use and they will learn a lot in the process of mixing the paint colours, etc.

We need to see that the process of a project is as important, if not more important, than the end result. We are on a learning journey where the final destination is only a part of the overall learning.

Collage writing but without the glue

Items readily found in an early years setting can also be used to form letters and write words, e.g. pine cones, counters, trucks and cars, shells. These are easily dismantled by the children when they no longer want them on display or want to change what they have 'written'.

Case study

The children were encouraged to bring in their favourite book and one child brought in *Hattie and the Fox*. After sharing the story, some of the children decided to play the game of hiding themselves and being found. They had parts to play. The fox did the hiding and the other animals reacted in different ways. This took a lot of discussion, reference back to the book itself and finding a suitable bush in the outdoor area. The children took it in turns to play the cow. They made a notice that said 'Moooo' and took turns to call out and frighten the fox away.

Plasticine writing

Given a piece of plasticine to work with, most children begin by moulding and stretching it into a worm-like length of stretchiness. This is then formed into many things: animals, flowers and, of course with maybe a little support, the first letter of their name.

Clay and air drying media make the final lettering permanent and can be decorated later with paint, glitter, sequins, paper and beads, varnished and used to decorate coat pegs, photo displays, etc.

Try to use different moulding media as they have different properties and densities and are suitable for the different stages of fine motor skills. Soft plasticine is less dense and more easily manipulated and thus more appropriate for very young children.

Clay requires greater strength and is therefore more appropriate for those children with greater finger and hand strength. Playing with these materials, however, strengthens hand muscles, dexterity and control and will be invaluable when children begin to hold and manipulate writing tools. In the meantime, they offer the chance to 'write' in a relaxed and informal environment without the pressure to hold and manipulate a pencil, brush, crayon or felt tip correctly in order to make marks.

Similarly, construction toys such as Lego can be used to 'write'. Reluctant writers (quite often boys) may enjoy writing with Lego or with sticks and stones on a path in the setting's outdoor area.

Writing with plants

Children love to see their name, or the initial letter of their name, especially in unusual places. When sowing seeds, consider sowing them in the form of the child's name. Seed cress grown on tissue in the shape of a child's initial name letter is fun.

Similarly, if you are growing vegetables such as marrows, pumpkins or squash in the setting's outdoor area consider carving a message such as 'Hello', 'Smile' or 'Look!' in the skin of a young vegetable and as it grows, the message will also grow.

Bedding plants and bulbs can be planted to form the word 'Welcome' or 'Hello' or the setting's name.

The children will enjoy pointing these words and letters out to family members as they arrive in your setting each morning.

Key questions

As writing with pens and pencils is the norm, using other tools and media will offer a different dimension to your writing activities. The following ideas will help you to consider a wider range of writing activities, situations that may arise and how you wish to consider your approach and generate an agreed working ethos.

- ☐ Are the resources easily accessible for the children to use independently? Are they attractively set out, well organised, well maintained and in sufficient numbers? Are they contributed to regularly in order to sustain interest and motivation?

- ☐ Do we see this as an important way of supporting learning about writing? Do we use the children's work in this area as evidence via photos, noting what they said during our observations? Do we formally include this area in our observation notes?

- ☐ Do we encourage the children to use several different media together or do we try to keep certain media to certain areas for reasons of tidiness? Are we confining creativity?

- ☐ Can children move freely to different areas to use other materials, refer to books and things they have seen in other parts of the setting to improve their work or are they 'encouraged' to 'stay here and finish what they are doing'.

- ☐ Do we have a problem-solving ethos in our setting? Do we discuss our work, what we want to do next, discuss suggestions and solutions to difficulties? Do we as educators become offended if our solution is not tried or adopted?

- ☐ Have we considered practicalities – do we daily discard the dried-up felt tips? Do we sharpen the pencils and crayons each day? Do the scissors cut all the papers we want them to cut? Does the glue really stick all the different paper and card weights we are expecting it to stick? There is nothing more frustrating than tools that do not do their job.

Notes

_____
_____
_____
_____
_____
_____
_____
_____
_____
_____
_____
_____
_____
_____
_____
_____
_____
_____

Links with the EYLF learning outcomes

Make a note of any evidence for the following elements you may observe:

1. Strong sense of identity

- Responds to ideas and suggestions from others
- Is open to new challenges and discoveries
- Increasingly cooperates and works collaboratively with others

2. Connected with and contributes to their world

- Understands different ways of collaborating through play and projects
- Is empowered to make choices and problem-solve to meet their needs in particular contexts
- Uses play to investigate, project and explore new ideas

3. A strong sense of wellbeing

- Increasingly cooperates and works collaboratively with others
- Recognises their individual achievements
- Manipulates equipment and manages tools with increasing competence and skill

4. Confident and involved learner

- Persists, even when they find a task difficult
- Manipulates objects and experiments with cause and effect, trial and error
- Makes connections between experiences, concepts and processes

5. Effective communicator

- Listens and responds to sounds and patterns in speech, stories and rhymes in context
- Is beginning to understand key literacy concepts and processes, such as the sound patterns of language, concepts of print and the ways texts are structured with a beginning, middle and end

3. Writing our name: a passport to literacy

'The writing of one's own name has, for many hundreds of years, been seen as a rite of passage towards literate behaviour' (Hall & Robinson 1995).

Children often use the letters in their name to move from mark-making to more formal writing. They will string together the letters from their name randomly but read those letters back to you as a complex sentence or story.

At first this story might change with each reading but as time goes on it will be the same story. The child has begun to understand that text carries meaning and educators will see that these are the very early stages of realising the purpose of texts. To anyone else, this is a string of random letters, albeit, those found in that particular child's name but to the writer they are a complete and meaningful text. When Rikki wrote her name she said, 'That's me and that's my name.'

Not only will the child be learning that print carries meaning, but also that the correct way to write English text is left to right, starting at the top of the page and progressing to the bottom. As they write they will be learning that they can write for different purposes too.

Some children are aware that writing is important and that a writer acquires some status. Thus learning to write one's name is very important and a gateway to learning further literacy skills. Correctly writing their name helps children to understand that letters have a specific order that does not change if it is to say their name on each occasion.

Paul was very proud to show that he could write his name, which he did at the top left-hand corner of his drawing page, writing from left to right. Then he turned round and said, 'I can do it the other way too!'

Learning to write one's name for its own sake can be a laborious task. But if children are writing their name for a reason – to label their work, to send a card to a sick friend or write a party invitation – then the process has purpose and meaning and most children aspire to make a good job of it.

One name, many different name cards

All children should have at least one name card readily accessible so that they can independently copy their name until such time when no prompt is needed. A starting dot and arrows, showing correct letter formation, can help as long as the children have had a little practice with an adult initially and know that these are merely aides and not a part of the letter itself.

Children should be encouraged to independently access their own name cards to label their work. There need to be several cards in different locations – at least one indoors and a laminated one outdoors. These should be made by the children with a little assistance to ensure accuracy so that when they later use them independently as prompts they are not copying and reinforcing earlier mistakes.

Here is Ella's change in her name writing over time, using capital letters to start with as these are easier to write at first – straight lines and circles.

Jessica sensed her 'e's were not right when she wrote her name (see the signing-in book on p. 26). One afternoon she was seen trying different forms of the letter 'e' at one of the easels.

Jessica called this her 'story of e' and she took it home with her. The next day, she went straight to the easel again to show what she had learned.

When a child has copied their name from their name card, they will be very proud of what they have achieved. To add interest, name cards can be written in various media, e.g. sandpaper or glitter, collaged and laminated, computer or hand written

Case study

When Kamal came to visit the primary school as part of an induction program of visits his teacher asked him if he was looking forward to coming to school. 'Yes,' he said. 'Cos then I'll be able to write like my sister in Mrs Smith's class.'

When Kamal later entered the Foundation year class his teacher learnt just how much he admired his older sister – the greater freedoms she enjoyed (playing out with friends, later bedtime, etc.) and her more advanced skills including being able to 'write properly' to which Kamal aspired.

Many children aspire to be like older siblings and writing their name is the first step, and indeed the rite of passage that Hall and Robinson (1995) write about.

Throughout the day children will have many occasions when they need to be able to write their name: to label and identify their work and belongings or to show when they have experienced a learning activity for example. Stephanie used a different colour for each letter of her name to match her painting.

Key questions

- [ ] When children bring in treasured possessions from home do you take time to acknowledge their 'treasure' and its value and explain that it should be labelled to ensure safe-keeping. Do you take a little time to help the child to label the item with their name, explaining how to write their name as you go? For example, 'Look there is an "S" at the beginning of your name. 'S for Sophie' etc. This is important because you are demonstrating that our writing does have a purpose.

- [ ] Can children readily access pre-cut labels on which they can write their names? Are these labels in a tray next to sharpened pencils, and other mark-making materials? Are laminated name labels also nearby so that the children can copy their names?

- [ ] Do you take time to ensure that the children are labelling their work? Do you also write their name if they are having difficulty, writing with the child rather than after they have left an area?

- [ ] Do you value a child's name writing, especially early mark-making, celebrating it and also writing the child's name so that another educator can read the name; thus making the child feel that their mark-making is successfully being read back?

- [ ] Do you have a special board to pin items that have not been named so that you can find the owner? Children will be upset if their work is lost and when it has been found you will be able to explain that their angst could have been avoided with a name label – again this is demonstrating that writing does have a purpose.

☐ Is there a 'signing-in' book available for the children as well as one for the parents? This will help you keep track of their learning and development over time as each page is dated.

Notes

_____
_____
_____
_____
_____
_____
_____
_____
_____
_____
_____
_____
_____
_____
_____
_____
_____
_____
_____
_____
_____
_____
_____
_____
_____
_____
_____
_____
_____
_____
_____

Links with the EYLF learning outcomes

Make a note of any evidence for the following elements you may observe:

1. Strong sense of identity

- Has a sense of the significance of their name
- Is beginning to explore the origins of their 'family' names
- Finds out if there are other children with the same name

2. Connected with and contributes to their world

- Shows an interest in the names of significant others
- Explores street names and the names of towns
- Writes a group letter to the council about an issue of importance

3. A strong sense of wellbeing

- Helps others who appear to have difficulty
- Approaches activities with confidence
- Shows excitement for a novel activity

4. Confident and involved learner

- Can locate and use resources appropriately
- Shows satisfaction in achievement
- Is keen to persist with a challenging activity

5. Effective communicator

- Is beginning to use their name to label their creations
- Identifies other children's names
- Uses their name in a made-up or favourite story

4. Writing on the run

The average under 5-year-old (if there is such a person) is a mobile being and that is how it should be. Sitting down quietly is anathema to them, sitting down quietly to write seems unreasonable when you are so young.

We find it difficult to show children that their mark-making has a purpose when we are not making it fit for their purpose but, rather, making their writing fit our purpose. We therefore feel that we have to adapt our writing opportunities to fit in with our children's 'busy-ness'. They need to be able to write on the run. To make jottings and take notes, and leave messages as they go. In order that they may do so effectively we need to offer writing stations that are mobile.

'It may be that some children prefer to read and write outside and get better results if they do' (Bilton 2013).

Treasure hunts and message trails

Children love hide and seek. They love the joy of hiding objects and finding objects. Finding foam letters in ice cubes will encourage writing with the letters and mark-making with the ice. Other items can be hidden in other messy media.

Treasure hunts involving searching for the letters in our names and objects that rhyme with those words that we are encountering in our storybook reading are more fun and more active than sitting down with paper, pen or a picture book.

Similarly, a set of post-it notes and a pencil with a leader child and educator sticking clues on a treasure hunt or message trail is fun and inspires many children to want to write and to want to read. Initially these trails will need support. Discuss the number of clues and where you will put them.

Then you can offer a 'message prompts' clipboard to support the game with a numbered picture or word clues for the children to copy and follow. Later the support board can offer ideas. Older children will be able to draw or write their own clues.

In its simplest form, a message trail can simply be a mark-making 'follow me' game where a child writes on a post-it note and sticks it on a tree, wall, bench and other children follow and have to copy the same pattern and stick it on the same tree, wall, bench, etc.

Mobile writing stations

The problem with writing is that many educators see it as a sedentary occupation whereas most young writers are on the move, and this is why many children are reluctant to initiate the activity as they feel their movement may be curtailed.

The pure joy of movement can be seen in every early years setting from the baby who has just learnt to 'cruise' along the furniture clinging on for dear life to the rambunctious 4-year-old hurling himself across the room to the resigned exclamations of 'Perhaps slow down' from the educator. It is hardly surprising then that for many young children writing just does not appeal, as they know that they will be required to sit still for what must feel like an extraordinarily long time.

Writing stations – which are dotted around the setting, easily accessed, and not requiring special equipment or seating – could be the answer, as well as writing bags, boxes and trays which make writing a mobile activity that can be enjoyed anywhere.

Have your own pencil case/post-it notes/ special pen/journal that you carry round – not just to make observation notes but to actually take time out to enjoy mark-making with the children.

Mobile writing stations such as trolleys, bags, boxes and trays enable children to add to the resources that have already been set up either by the educators or by the children. When children have ownership of the activity they tend to benefit more.

Resource ideas for mobile writing stations

- Buckets with assorted brushes – label the buckets with a pictorial and written sign 'fill with water' and this bucket can be used outdoors for water painting walls and windows
- Containers with rolls of paper, assorted large felt markers and wax crayons
- Push-along trolleys holding similar stationery found on the indoor and outdoor writing tables, e.g. chalk, felt tips, pens, pencils, rubbers, rulers, hole punches, crayons, card, a variety of paper – tracing paper, lined, squared etc., stickers, stamps and ink pads
- A couple of easels dotted around your room with paper set up and crayons or felt tips and paper set ready with a label 'Can you draw what you can see?' This may inspire some observational drawing and a dictated written caption. Children will find this much easier to access independently than a painting easel.

- Wheelbarrow with plant pots, seed packets, envelopes for DIY seed envelopes, crayons, pencils, plant labels, watering cans, pack of compost for the digging area outdoors
- Children's novelty/character lunch boxes with handles or small plastic DIY tool boxes with carry handles holding a selection of stationery as above
- Themed and novelty birthday cards and stationery (bought cheaply in the $2 shop or printed from the computer) to make up themed writing bags. For instance, if appropriate, a princess writing bag with fluffy trimmed pens and tiara, a builder's toolbox with measuring tape, toy hammers, screwdrivers, pencils, paper and hard hat, a doctor's/nurse's/vet's medicine bag with stethoscope, thermometer, prescription pad and patient notes.

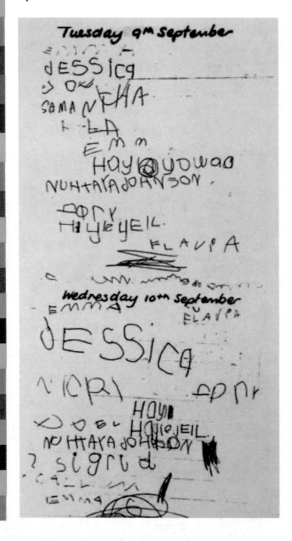

- If your setting still has a 'signing in' time you will probably find that the children will love to have their own signing in book. Set up a small space in the room with an A4 book and a pen. If you put all these in a basket with a handle then the signing in can be done anywhere in the setting. You can put a storybook in the basket too, as many children have to wait their turn. Below you can see the full range of name writing capabilities from one group of children.

Trolleys can be pushed and pulled, emptied and filled. Bags and boxes can be filled and emptied. Trays can be filled, emptied and their contents arranged and rearranged. This is what some children might choose to do with your carefully considered resources. Not a letter or word may be written.

It's also important to realise that we provide resources as a starting point for children's activities. We may have a plan with teaching intentions that we want children to be responding to, but within the settings we are helping to create scenarios *with* not *for* the children. And this includes our involvement in all areas of learning including writing.

'All an adult needs to remember if the play is to be deep and rich in quality, is that their play agenda is no more important than that of the other players' (Bruce 2004).

Case study

The educator sat down at the writing table one day to write herself a quick note to remind her that a child was being collected by a different family member that evening. As she put the note in her pocket she asked a child at the writing table if he liked the new 'magic' felt tips that changed colour if you wrote on them with one of the pens. He said they were brilliant and invited her to have a go, telling the educator which were his favourite colours, so she sat and experimented, soon attracting an interested crowd.

If we want children to want to write, then they must see the benefits of writing. They must see that it has a purpose, but most of all they need to see that it is an enjoyable experience. You are the key to this. Writing for a purpose is an important part of our learning about writing. Writing for pleasure should be an important part of our writing lives.

Key questions

Writing is traditionally considered to be a sedentary occupation. The following points might help you to ensure that quality writing is still taking place.

- ☐ Do the writing activities still offer valid writing opportunities? Can you offer more than just a notebook and pencil?
- ☐ Do the activities relate to what they are contained, for example in gardening or building writing activities in a wheelbarrow?
- ☐ Do you regularly check that the writing resources are still within each writing area – are they in good condition?
- ☐ Are we encouraging the children to build stories and role-play scenarios around these writing resources? Do we talk to them in character, encouraging them to take on a role and draw and compose in that role?
- ☐ Are we offering sufficient support so that there is some writing on the run and not merely lots of running?

Notes

_____
_____
_____
_____
_____
_____
_____
_____
_____

Links with the EYLF learning outcomes

Make a note of any evidence for the following elements you may observe:

1. Strong sense of identity

- Considers the consequences of their words and actions for themselves and others
- Explores aspects of identity through mark-making and drawing
- Recognises their individual achievements as well as the achievements of others

2. Connected with and contributes to their world

- Looks closely at similarities, differences, patterns and change
- Notices print and its purposes in their community
- Is becoming aware that not all writing scripts are the same (e.g. Arabic, Chinese)

3. A strong sense of wellbeing

- Is confident to try new activities
- Selects and uses resources independently
- Makes choices and accepts challenges

4. Confident and involved learner

- Expresses wonder and interest
- Follows and extends their own interests with enthusiasm, energy and concentration
- Creates and uses representation to organise, record and communicate ideas and concepts

5. Effective communicator

- Conveys and constructs messages with purpose and confidence
- Actively uses and engages with and shares enjoyment of language and texts in a range of ways
- Is beginning to be aware of the relationship between oral, written and visual representations

5. Writing opportunities within the daily routine

'Writing begins to develop when children make their first marks and the development of writing begins when children have access to implements such as textas, media such as paint and different surfaces' (Palmer, Bayley & Raban 2014, p. 92).

Each day, within the routine of the setting, there are many writing opportunities. Children see us writing and many will want to copy what we are doing. We have all been asked what we are doing when we make lists, write observation post-it notes, etc. Try to have a set of similar child-friendly stationery for your children to use.

We are always surprised how children just love playing at being the educator. Try to make such role-play opportunities as mobile as possible – an open basket entices the child more than a closed bag, and if it has a carry handle it can be easily transported indoors or out. Flexible, plastic baskets are very child friendly as they are lightweight when empty and come in a variety of sizes. They are also very colourful, and easy on restricted budgets.

As you assess the children's use of free flow areas such as different role-play areas and the snack area, encourage them to independently tick their name off against that activity once they have done it.

Diaries

Encourage children to take photos of their day, which they can annotate in a shared diary. Similarly, an assessment record of their stay in your setting can be a joint effort if both you and the child record observations of their experiences including photographs, artwork and writing.

A big book diary completed at the end of a session with a photo and note of what has happened that day, written by children and educators, fascinates children and is often returned to as children find a sense of security in going back days later to 'read' what has happened before. For younger children, this is security in the sense of 'belonging' but for older children who are learning about reading

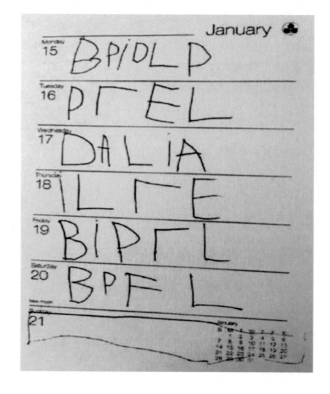

and writing, this can also be security in the knowledge that there is a page or two in the diary that they can 'read' and enjoy all by themselves.

If any members of staff are reluctant to embrace the idea of diaries, the last line of persuasion can always be that they offer excellent evidence of good practice and are a readily available record of experiences. But hopefully the children's enjoyment, whilst advancing their understanding about writing, will be reason enough to embark on the journal writing journey.

Personal journals – formal and informal

For children with additional needs, specialists such as an educational psychologist or speech therapist visiting the setting can get a picture of the child's learning experience before they start to work with the child. Families can also share these profiles and add their own observations. When children move to a new setting, these profiles should go with them so that an easier transition can be facilitated.

It's important for a child to contribute to his or her record of their experiences and that it's in the form of a personal journal that the child has a sense of 'ownership' over. Try to keep these profile journals readily available in the setting so that both you and the children can readily suggest activities that can be documented.

Encourage children to take photographs to put into their journals as a visual record of their achievements. What goes into the profile should be negotiated as far as possible and each new success that is recorded against the journey achieving the EYLF learning outcomes should be celebrated together.

A collaborative noticeboard

When you invite your children to participate in the upkeep of your room's noticeboard you take a giant leap of faith into the world of cooperative 'writing'. You have encouraged unconditional participation and therefore must accept with a smile that the noticeboard might never again be a pristine vision of colour-coordinated beauty.

Try to overlook any imperfections that appear and look the other way rather than correct or 'tweak' anything that does not seem quite right to your educator's eye. It's so easy to damage the aspiring writer's confidence. If you feel unable to stop yourself altering and editing then it's better not to have a shared noticeboard, which would be a shame because it can be an excellent way of encouraging children, educators and families to share 'ownership' of their setting and its daily life.

In order to maintain a little order you could divide the board with paper borders and ask the children to help you to write headings such as 'Dates to remember', 'Items for sale', 'Wanted', 'Lost and found', 'This week's news'.

It's welcoming to add a section for 'special things' where families can share aspects of their culture, religion or family life. This might be a photo of a first communion, a child's Bar mitzvah, Diwali celebrations, the photo announcement of a new baby, etc. – all special times to share and talk about are good conversation openers for family members as they drop off and collect their children.

This can also serve as a resource board of fun, inexpensive things to do in your local area for young children and their families.

You could also have a table under the noticeboard for spontaneous artwork, and items of interest that the children have made or found either in the setting or at home. Here everyone can contribute an item with a brief description if they wish. If family members are busy or in a rush, offer to write the description of the child's 'treasure' with them or find treasures with the children in the setting so that no-one feels excluded by time pressure.

These activities foster a sense of belonging, not only for your children but also for the educators and for the families in your setting. It will help to encourage feelings of purpose and belonging as well as involvement in a joint writing project.

Display boards

There are other types of display boards that encourage group writing. Once again, these collaborative writing efforts are fun and may not result in neatly presented boards but they do encourage a sustained writing interest. One group of children decided to make a notice of some rules for their room: 'Don't muck about' and 'Don't pick your nose'.

To ensure that the boards maintain aspects of child-initiated writing, resources should be readily available nearby and you need to remind the children of the kinds of things that they could be 'writing' about. When a child has made a model to be proud of, remind them that they could make a name label for it and put it on the display table for everyone to see. Or ask them if they would like to take a photo and label it before they print it out and pin it on the display board.

As children begin to label their own work and contribute to display boards you may find that they extend this 'ownership' by making display banners, signposts, flags and larger labels of welcome. Here are some ideas for collaborative display boards.

A day in our room

Children can take photos and annotate a typical day, an outing or special times of the day – particularly useful for children who find transitions difficult to manage.

Annotated picture timetable

During the day, ask the children to take photos with you of the different activities that are going on and a photo of the clock showing the time these activities are happening.

Include shots of children entering your room, families leaving and then coming back at the end of the session to collect the children and the children finally leaving. Seeing pictures of their family and friends coming back for them and then themselves actually leaving the premises gently reminds homesick children of the natural order of things and that they will soon see familiar faces from home.

Ask the children to help download, print and compile these into a picture timetable. This will help children with their writing and mark-making skills but also with their early reading abilities.

Picture timetables encourage children to be aware of the passing of time and how they will be spending this time in your room. Many children find it comforting to know what will come next rather than to have the next activity suddenly sprung upon them. Similarly, most children find transition times easier to deal with if they have had a little warning.

Rather than merely being told it's tidy up time, it seems fairer to warn children that it's time to begin to wind down their game as it will soon be time to tidy up. Offer opportunities to save their models, painting, collage, etc. to be continued later. Have as little tidying away as possible so that activities are disrupted as little as possible and can be returned to and continued.

Joke board

Encourage children to write a joke on a post-it note and stick it on the joke board. As a background to the board, have a large laminated child's joke that everybody understands.

You will get lots of jokes that aren't jokes, aren't funny, have no punch line and are merely a narrative as your children begin to understand what a joke is, how to remember one and then how to deliver it! And then when they can finally deliver a funny joke you will be inundated with all manner of cheesy old jokes. But that laminated joke will keep you all going in the meantime.

'Memphis says' board

Place a laminated speech bubble next to a picture of a favourite character or a child in the group. Children can then write in the speech bubble what they think the character is saying using whiteboard marker pens. Several of these can offer a storyboard for the children to record conversations that may have taken place in the current chosen stories e.g. *Possum Magic* or *Rosie's Walk*.

It's fun to draw around a child and have a life size character and then the laminated speech bubble can be large enough to accommodate the children's writing. Put a pocket on the character's clothing to hold the marker pens and a cloth for wiping away the writing, ready for children to independently write in the speech bubble.

News board

Encourage educators, children and families to add their own snippets of news: birthdays, new babies, milestones reached, etc.

'In case I forget' message board

Let the children write memos on a whiteboard near your chair – things you must remember – e.g. letters to go home, or the name of a child leaving early that day or being collected by a different person than usual.

Clipboard surveys

Some children are familiar with market research surveys and are generally very interested in what their friends think about things.

Case study

How do you feel today?

The educators at a preschool had noticed that children who had previously appeared to be quite settled in the setting were finding it difficult to separate from their parents each morning and were becoming tearful.

Several parents had disclosed to the educators that the children were experiencing difficulties at home with parents splitting up. One child had been bereaved whilst several others had recently moved house. It was unusual for so much transition to be occurring at the same time. It was impossible to predict from one day to another how the children were going to be.

The director set up a 'How do you feel today?' board and all the children drew a face showing how they were feeling that day – happy, sad, giggly, mischievous (most copied the mischievous face, forgetting what it meant but liking the sound of the word). The educators liked this direct way of asking the children how they were feeling that day and it did work; such was the level of emotion being experienced by these young children.

Gradually the board became a clipboard survey and the children went round asking each other how they felt that day.

Over time, new surveys were carried out:

'What did you have for breakfast?'

'What's your favourite story?'

'What's your favourite dinner?'

'What's your favourite game?'

The children loved asking each other questions, enjoyed noting down the answers and the possibilities were seemingly endless. Surveys became a permanent part of the room's mark-making fun.

Weather station survey

Most children love being outdoors in all weathers. Many children we have taught enjoyed keeping weather records. Cut out and laminate pictures of clouds, the sun, rain, strong winds, etc. The children will make selections for the day and chose the corresponding word to describe the day's weather.

Resource ideas for your weather station

- Container to catch and measure rainfall
- Weather vane and windsocks
- Outdoor thermometer
- Indoor barometer
- Weather chart
- Camera
- Weather diary to describe the weather, record rainfall figures and temperature and feature pictures of your setting in different weather conditions and seasons
- Simple non-fiction books about the weather
- Access to online weather forecast (www.bom.com.au)

Don't forget numbers

Just as writing is synonymous with mark-making and finger painting, writing also covers writing both letters and numbers.

Ideas for writing activities involving numbers

- Children can write their own labels for the number of children who can be at any one time in an area, e.g. '4 children can be here' with four smiley faces labelled 1, 2, 3 and 4.
- In surveys, children can add a mark-making tally and the final total.
- Show children how to make their own chalked hopscotch frame in the outdoor area.

- Make a chalked number snake outside on the path or a numbered ladder on a wall – this can then be linked to playing a snakes and ladders game outdoors with other activities with a snakes and ladders theme, e.g. a snakes and ladders obstacle course.
- An activity course with skipping ropes, hoola hoops, beanbags with a number sign written by the children indicating how many times they must skip, hoola, throw and catch before moving on to the next activity.
- Count how many children are in the preschool each morning and a different monitor each day records the number.

Key questions

Every day is a rich writing opportunity. Are we making the most of this daily resource? Accommodating ad hoc writing opportunities is not easy especially in the rush of a hectic day. The following questions may help us to think about incorporating more writing opportunities into each day.

- ☐ Have we discussed, as a team, the frustrations we may encounter as we explore, with the children, the writing opportunities within our daily routine? Displays, journals and profiles may not be as neat as they once were. Are we comfortable with this?
- ☐ Have we discussed the importance of the process of writing as well as the product of that writing not only amongst the room team but also with families?
- ☐ Do we encourage and praise the children as they write, as well as when they have completed a piece of writing or mark-making?
- ☐ Do we support the children to decide what and how to write?
- ☐ How much of the writing in our room is child-initiated and how much is educator-directed?

☐ How much of the writing on display in our setting has been written by an educator and how much by a child? Do the children ask you to scribe to their drawings?

Links with the EYLF learning outcomes

Make a note of any evidence for the following elements you may observe:

1. Strong sense of identity

- Uses effective routines to help make predicted transitions smooth
- Senses and responds to a feeling of belonging
- Uses their home language to construct meanings

2. Connected with and contributes to their world

- Is beginning to understand and evaluate ways in which texts are used to construct identities and create stereotypes
- Participates collaboratively in everyday routines
- Takes opportunities to contribute to decisions

3. A strong sense of wellbeing

- Seeks out and accepts new challenges, makes new discoveries and celebrates their own achievements and those of others
- Combines fine (and gross) motor movement (and balance) to achieve increasingly complex patterns

- Experiences and shares personal successes in learning and initiates opportunities for new learning in their home language and in English.

4. Confident and involved learner

- Experiments with different technologies
- Uses feedback from themselves and others to build on and revise an idea
- Makes predictions and generalisations about their daily activities, aspects of the natural world and environment using patterns they generate or identify, and communicates these using mathematical language and symbols

5. Effective communicator

- Shows increasing knowledge, understanding and skill in conveying meaning in at least one language
- Takes on roles of literacy and numeracy users in their play
- Uses language and engages in play to imagine and create roles, scripts and ideas

Notes

_____
_____
_____
_____
_____
_____
_____
_____
_____
_____
_____
_____
_____
_____
_____
_____
_____
_____

6. Maintaining an inviting writing area

'If children are to begin to see themselves as writers it is essential that we provide them with opportunities and resources' (Palmer, Bayley & Raban 2014, p. 103)

All settings now have a writing table – an area where the children know that they can readily and independently access a wide variety of stationery and writing implements that will cover all their needs. It's important that this area is monitored each day so that it is always well stocked and attractive. Ideally, it should also be the area where educators come for their own writing needs. Children should know that they must return items after use and that they need to keep the area tidy so that it is always pleasant and ready to be used by the next person.

Ensure that there is a bin for unwanted drafts nearby and that there is a display pinboard so that treasured writing can be displayed.

To ensure that interest is maintained, try to add new and interesting items each week.

Resources to include in the writing area

- A variety of paper – lined, unlined, square, tracing, post-it notes. Offer more coloured paper than white paper as this seems to be more inspiring.
- Shaped paper – stars, hearts, animals, etc. When putting up a display use the off-cuts of backing paper and old backing paper you have recently removed and cut into different shapes – cloud shapes for 'I wish ...' writing frames, a smiley mouth for 'I like ...' frames, etc.
- Printed stationery – either bought cheaply or printed using clipart from your computer and then photocopied
- Pens, pencils, felt tips, crayons, chalks, wax crayons and pastels for resistance 'magic' writing. (To avoid the problem of missing tops from pens you can glue the tops to a piece of wood or along a ruler and then the children simply replace the pen – no searching under the table for the top. This also avoids the temptation to put pen tops in their mouths.)
- Paper clips
- Hole punch
- Stapler
- Diaries, notepads, address books, invitations, greetings cards and postcards
- Stickers, stamps and ink-pads
- Raffle ticket books
- Pipe-cleaners and plasticine to fashion into letters. These offer writing opportunities and the chance to build finger strength and fine motor skills.
- A magnetic board and plastic letters
- Labels, files and folders.
- Calendars
- A phone – talking often inspires 'writing' and notes need to be taken
- Scissors, glue stick, sticky tape, Blu-tack and masking tape
- Rulers
- Erasers
- Post box and postage stamps

- Clipboards with pencils attached
- Writing prompts, including name cards, alphabet charts and an invitation to write
- Make your own writing frames to suit the children's interests and hobbies. Photocopy a relevant picture, leaving a small space for writing – small spaces to start with as they are less intimidating to fill.
- Try to have a similar area outside or a trolley holding similar resources that can be taken outdoors.

Resources to include in an outside area:

- 'Artist's studio' with easels, books and paintings of famous artists, adult painting media, e.g. tubes of watercolours with palette trays as well as the usual children's paints
- Outdoor water painting area
- A place for wax crayon etching
- Floor chalking space

Motivate children to write by having an 'I can write' display board next to your writing table. Take photos of the children writing and add it to the board. It will inspire children to have a go so that they too can have their photo taken and added to the display.

A birthday table

Encourage card-making – children can make birthday cards to give to family, pets and friends. They can make bunting and paper hats using scissors and sticky tape. Making plasticine cakes will strengthen fingers and encourage fine motor skills. Add birthday cake candles and their tiny holders as this will improve coordination and dexterity.

A messy table

This is not for the faint hearted! A wipe-clean table is needed outdoors or in an area with a wipe-clean floor. Add media directly to the table that the children can 'write' directly into with their fingers, e.g. finger paints, soap flakes, coffee granules, food colouring, glitter sprinkles or a combination of these things. Make the consistency fairly thick to facilitate easier mark-making and less mess.

Extendable writing and writing walls

Some children are fascinated by the extending capability of a roll of paper on the floor and will often spend a long time trying to 'fill up' the space with their mark-making.

A paper roll can be used on the floor or perhaps the easier option is to secure it to the wall at child height. With this option though, the onus is on you to remind them on a daily basis that it is fine to 'write' on this special 'writing wall' in our room but it is not appropriate to 'write' on any of the walls in their own homes or at their grandparent's homes.

Date each new piece of paper and annotate what the children tell you about their mark-making, as this will give you an insight into their interests and their growing imagination. Write their names for them if they are unable to do so as this gives them 'ownership' of their work and makes them keen to show visitors as well as family and friends what they have done.

As each piece of paper is completed, do not remove it from the wall, simply add a fresh layer on top. After several months you will have a comprehensive planning and assessment writing record should anyone ask for one which, no doubt, someone will.

Rolls of paper are fun to take outdoors though you may want to cut them into more manageable lengths. Again they can be fixed to walls or simply rolled along the ground.

Paper attached to brick walls can be used to take wax crayon rubbings of the brickwork. Similarly, paper can be attached to tree trunks, pathways and other textured surfaces to get similar effects. Blackboards, magnetic letter boards, collage boards, whiteboards and interactive whiteboards all offer 'writing wall' opportunities. Care has to be taken that they are at the right height for all children to access, that writing implements are readily available and that the right pens are used with each board. Mistakes are expensive on interactive boards but this should not stop free independent access.

We know this may sound obvious but never underestimate the use of a coloured paper for livening up an activity that has been used before and may have lost some of its initial impact. Use of bright coloured paper often makes the activity seem like new again and renews interest, especially if children are invited to choose the colour.

Key questions

Writing areas can very easily become tired looking and jaded. We need to not only maintain them but to model their use. If we are not inspired to use them, then we cannot expect our children to want to use them. The following questions may help us to consider the writing area and its use from the children's point of view.

- ☐ Do we have designated mark-making/writing areas in our room – both indoors and outdoors where both educators and children can find all the writing implements they require?
- ☐ Are the writing areas easy to access independently?
- ☐ Do we have sufficient resources for all the children, e.g. different thicknesses of pens, pencils and crayons to accommodate different fine motor skills and pencil control?
- ☐ Do we check each day that dried-up felt tips are thrown away and pencils and crayons sharpened?
- ☐ Each week do we put something new into the area to sustain interest and motivation?
- ☐ Do we ensure that the resources are good quality? Do we include 'real life' resources: diaries, suitable invoices, appropriate letter headings, bank slips, etc.

- ☐ Do we take time to sit with the children and enjoy writing with them, modelling how to write, talking about our writing, what we are doing and how we write, so that some of the mystery is taken away?

- ☐ Do we support the children to make their own special occasion cards, or are they expected to make a card that we have offered as an example that must be copied.

Notes

_____
_____
_____
_____
_____
_____
_____
_____
_____
_____
_____
_____
_____
_____
_____
_____
_____
_____
_____
_____
_____
_____
_____
_____
_____
_____
_____

Links with the EYLF learning outcomes

Make a note of any evidence for the following elements you may observe:

1. Strong sense of identity

- Celebrates and shares their contributions and achievements with others
- Shows interest in other children and being part of a group
- Engages in and contributes to shared play experiences

2. Connected with and contributes to their world

- Cooperates with others and negotiates roles and relationships in play
- Is beginning to think critically about fair and unfair behaviour
- Takes action to assist other children to participate in social groups

3. A strong sense of wellbeing

- Engages in new activities with confidence and optimism
- Perseveres in the face of difficulty
- Integrates sensory, motor and cognitive networks

4. Confident and involved learner

- Initiates and contributes to play experiences emerging from their own ideas
- Applies generalisations from one situation to another
- Explores the purpose and function of a range of tools, media, sounds and graphics

5. Effective communicator

- Draws on their experiences in constructing meaning using symbols
- Engages with technology for fun and to make meanings
- Develops an understanding that symbols are a powerful means of communication and that ideas, thoughts and concepts can be represented through them

7. Writing and creative development

'Children's learning is dynamic, complex and holistic. Physical, social, emotional, personal, spiritual, creative, cognitive and linguistic aspects of learning are all intricately interwoven and interrelated' (EYLF p. 9).

When we work creatively we are able to see connections with things we have learnt before, and our children are able to make connections between different areas of the program too. Working creatively also helps us with problem-solving. This is invaluable when we are trying to learn something that may not come easily to us or which may need a lot of practice. Many of us, though not all of us, find creative activities pleasurable and even relaxing, which can thus enhance the learning experience.

It would therefore seem reasonable to suppose that writing can, and indeed should, be experienced alongside the creative learning and development of the EYLF.

Writing and cooking

The way to a child's writing heart can be via their stomach, though you may only want to encourage this occasionally. Whilst we must all be health conscious and promote healthy living to the children in our care, we think that most educators are very aware that children love their food and love learning that involves the preparation, cooking and eating of that food. When the home corner was resourced as a cafe, the children wrote and illustrated menus.

Reluctant readers and writers suddenly become much more interested in reading and writing when food is involved. Reading and writing cooking magazines, cookery books recipe cards, menus, shopping ingredient lists and the preparation for cooking sessions that will actually be carried out, offer reward and incentive.

Cooking sessions need to be carried out soon after the writing preparation as young children will find it difficult to comprehend writing a shopping list for something that will be cooked at a later date, even the following day.

Any writing and shopping needs to be done early on in the session so that the food preparation and/or cooking can be completed in the same session, otherwise the child will feel cheated and any incentive will be lost for next time you plan to include writing with a food related activity.

Writing need not be limited to recording menus and recipes. Low fat/low sugar biscuits and cakes could be pre-baked as part of a math's activity and intentional teaching about volume and capacity, weighing and measuring. In the follow-up session children could ice them with their initials or words that are important to them, using icing pens.

Alphabet and number moulds and cutters could be used to make savoury biscuits and sandwiches for snack time and lunches.

You can also hold food taste tests where a variety of food samples are set out and the children record their favourite foods using simple tick or smiley face charts. This can be linked to healthy food programs, e.g. favourite fruits, vegetables.

Enriching the process with role-play

There should always be writing opportunities in the role-play area that are subject linked to the role-play scenario – jotter pads for lists, phone message boards, clipboards, signing-in books, diaries, address books, etc. On one occasion the role-play area was set up as a police station, with writing equipment and police officer's note books.

As well as the role-play area that links with the planned topic, one educator always had a role-play area next to her chair where the children gathered for music time, story time and home time. Here she kept a basket with blank pages for the children to use with a pen, some story books, stickers, mini whiteboard and marker pens, a story for story time, and 'Notes for families' which 'the educator' can write.

The children knew this was their basket and that they could climb on to the chair and be the educator – beware you may see yourself through your children's eyes!

However, this was also a good way to see what they were learning as they often rehearsed learning situations they had been previously practicing such as reading, writing or counting techniques. Any misconceptions could be noted by the educator and addressed sympathetically there and then. Sometimes, so as not to break the flow of an activity, a note was made in the planning to address any misconceptions in the whole group sessions soon afterwards.

Letter writing

As children become more accustomed to writing and when they are also forming opinions about favourite book and television characters you might like to add simple letter writing frames to your writing table. A picture of their favourite character with 'Dear ...' on a piece of writing paper will often inspire a letter or two.

Erin only knew well the letters in her own name, but when she wrote to her educator she used these letters in different orders to say different words:

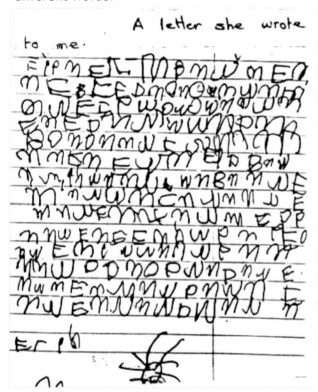

We realised how fascinated children were by letter writing when a child in our group was ill and we wrote to her. Her mother encouraged her to write back. Letters happily bobbed back and forth and this quickly became our most popular activity and child-initiated at that. When the child returned, we were concerned how all that spontaneous writing could be maintained. This child's absence had opened our eyes to how much the children had enjoyed letter writing.

Adding writing opportunities to favourite activities

Children often offer a commentary as they engage in an activity, telling you what they are doing, talking to the other children or the toys involved. Sometimes this is a way of controlling their actions and explaining the rules of their game to the other children.

Sometimes this commentary is copying what they might have seen in other areas of their lives – in television sports commentary for instance. Without interfering with the flow, these commentaries can be successfully recorded by the children.

Provide a 'goal score' blackboard and chalks in a play area together with a microphone for a 'match of the day' type commentary. This could be extended for older children with a match report for the whole group delivered from a cardboard box television screen. For written sports journalism, children can record their races and games with photos and writing.

Put a clipboard in the pet area so children can write feeding instructions, log when they fed the animals or add a note for the next person who feeds them.

Put together lengths of fabric to wrap and drape as clothes as well as the usual dressing up ensemble. Include sewing pattern books. Encourage children to draw their designs. Would the children enjoy drawing simple patterns for doll's clothes that they can then make? Simple T shapes make good tops for action figures and baby dolls alike and rectangles make hats and scarves. Fabric pens can be used to decorate fabric swatches as well as T-shirts, T-towels, etc. Paper dolls with paper clothes could also be made and decorated.

A roll of paper and pens in the construction area helps the children to make their own car mats, road maps, farms and train tracks.

When they are involved in a cooking activity, children can write a recipe or menu card and a taste test card with smiley faces or sad faces indicating whether the resulting food is tasty enough to cook again.

Children often enjoy visiting the office and many office staff enjoy their visits too. 'Helping in the office' can be a fun activity if office staff enjoy having a small group of young visitors. This works well if children are given small tasks that involve writing during their visit. Children can then set up a role-play 'office' in the home corner.

If you are working from your own home can you encourage children to take a note for you – shopping you may need when items are used up at snack time or a note about a phone call received?

Case study

On a small table, a small letter-writing tray with paper, envelopes, sticker 'stamps', assorted pens and felt tips was set up, and together with the children, we made a letter box in which we could 'post' our letters. On a walk to our letter box at the end of the road we noticed that letters were collected at certain times of the day and we decided on set collection and delivery times for our own letter box.

The children took it in turns to be post person setting up their own rota on a clipboard and ticking their name off when they had had a turn. All of this they managed to self-direct after the first couple of adult-assisted turns.

When the educators were out and about at weekends we began to pop a postcard in the letter-box wherever we were. If we forgot, we printed a photo of the place we had visited (sometimes from the internet) on to card and made it into a postcard and posted that, sometimes via Australia Post in the box at the end of the street and sometimes in our own room letter-box.

The logistics didn't really matter – the children just loved getting a letter, reading something that was written especially for them and, more importantly, these postcards inspired them and their family members to send postcards to our setting when they were on their travels. These could be from our local town, when they visited the nearby theme park or the town's library.

A postcard

DEQA 2IMON
I'm having lots of sleepovers.
I U U

Simon and Jackie
New Zealand

Writing to music

'Use language and representations from play, music and art to share and project meaning' (EYLF, p. 40).

Background music in the room is calming for both educators and children. However, it can also be used as a prop for writing – inspiring fluency for free flow mark-making when practicing pen control is one of your teaching intentions and simply enjoying the large movements that can be made and the fun that can be had.

As the tone, beat and rhythm of a piece changes so can the marks being made and each crescendo can create a collage of different writing marks and styles. Even reluctant writers can get quite carried away, offering prolific pieces of work while enjoying this relaxed writing form.

Cover a table with paper and the children can collect their favourite mark-making equipment. They can then mark-make/write in time to the music of a favourite song. You could also write to music by mark-making with finger paints on the table and then pressing the finished design on to larger sheets of paper.

Ideas for music you could use

- A nursery rhyme CD, e.g. drawing the *Grand Old Duke of York* and his men marching up and down the hill or *Humpty Dumpty* sitting on his wall.

- Classical music enables more spontaneous mark-making in time to the music. You can choose whether or not you offer any explanation of the music title, e.g. Korsakov's *The Flight of the Bumble Bee* or Prokofiev's *Peter and The Wolf.*

- Favourite character theme tunes could also be used or favourite seasonal songs.

Writing our own books

From the very first day children arrive in our settings we share books with them. It seems reasonable that very soon after, we should begin to make our own books and share those at story time too.

When children see you taking photos, annotating them, sticking them together, laminating the book – all the different stages of book making – they will invariably want to be involved. If you leave resources out for them they will want to try the more child-friendly elements themselves.

If you show you welcome their lead they will be happy to ask you to help with the more necessary aspects such as laminating. In one Indigenous community, the Elders told the children stories that they wrote in language and the educator wrote them in English as well. The educator invited the children to illustrate the stories and she laminated these books for the children to read:

Books can be about anything and everything:

- Our own version of a favourite book
- A big book of the people in our setting
- A group diary of our day
- A 'working' diary with dates to remember such as outings, visitors, birthdays, etc. Ask children to add to these each day.
- A trip

- Where we live – an address book with photos of our houses, pictures of local shops, library, bus stop, school, etc.
- Our room book – showing the children's annotated photographs
- 'Things I like in our setting' book with photos and annotations
- Our birthday book – dates of birthdays, the birthday person and how you celebrate a birthday in your setting
- Our pets
- Special interest books are also fun to make. Non-fiction books about our hobbies, interests, pets, etc. are personal to us and possibly more interesting and relevant to read and may engage some of our usually less interested 'readers' and 'writers'.

Children love to hear stories where they are the main characters. They can help to write these stories and take photographs of themselves to illustrate the book. They can also make up their own stories using storyboards and story boxes (shoes boxes with story puppets and props) and you can help compile these stories by acting as their scribe and taking photographs.

Children find it easier to write stories if they have played a part in story telling – making up and acting out stories of their own. We can help to record these stories and make them into exciting big books, which the children will enjoy helping to 'write' and later 'read'.

Making books

Children may want to make their own books. Have some folded paper on your writing table propped up with a label inviting the children to make a book. Offer a prop sample with stickers of a favourite book character and a simply written page. A piece of paper folded over is a good start as there is less blank paper to fill – no writer's block to overcome at the first attempt.

Concertina books are fun. These can be the standard rectangular concertina books but these can also be cut into shapes, e.g. boys and girls holding hands in a line ready for mark-making.

Children recognise the initial letter in their name early on in their reading and writing so will enjoy a book that has their initial letter on the front cover or a book in the shape of the letter. Simply cut out the letter in several differently coloured pieces of paper and staple them together either at the left hand side or at the top to make a flip-over book.

Children love to hear stories where they are the main characters. They can help to write these stories and take photographs of themselves to illustrate the book.

They can also make up their own stories using storyboards and story boxes (shoe boxes with story puppets and props) and you can help compile these stories by acting as their scribe and taking photographs.

Later, and for older children, have a selection of homemade books ready to be filled on your writing tables. Folded and stapled paper makes an instant ready-to-use book as does a strip of paper folded concertina style. Gradually children will simply make their own books up anyway but these simple ready made books will give them a start. Again, don't include too many blank pages as this may be a little off-putting.

Key questions

Many of us learn more if our learning is within a creative context, yet many of us claim not to be creative. The following questions will help us to reflect upon how we consider our own and other's creativity, how that links to learning and how we can convey that to others.

- ☐ Have we considered sufficiently, as a team, how children can develop their writing skills via creativity? Are we confident in expressing this knowledge to the children's families?

- ☐ Do we place as much importance on the process as we do on the end product?

- ☐ Do we consider some children to be more creative than others?

- ☐ Do we have a restricted view of what is 'creative'?

- ☐ How much autonomy do we give to children within the area of creativity? Do the children make decisions about what materials to use? Do we interfere too much? Are we concerned if something does not look like an accurate representation?

- ☐ When creativity is not tidy do we feel uncomfortable?

- ☐ Does a writing activity have to be a quiet and tidy activity?

Notes

_____

_____

_____

_____

_____

_____

_____

_____

_____

_____

_____

Links with the EYLF Learning Outcomes

Make a note of any evidence for the following elements you may observe:

1. Strong sense of identity
- Takes considered risk in their decision-making and copes with the unexpected
- Approaches new, safe situations with confidence
- Shares aspects of their culture with other children and educators

2. Connected with and contributes to their world
- Becomes aware of connections, similarities and differences between people
- Discovers and explores some connections among people
- Shows growing appreciation and care for natural and constructed environments

3. A strong sense of wellbeing
- Shares humour, happiness and satisfaction
- Acknowledges and accepts affirmation
- Is happy, healthy, safe and connected to others

4. Confident and involved learner
- Explores their environment
- Tries out strategies that were effective to solve problems in one situation to another
- Engages in learning relationships

5. Effective communicator
- Recognises and engages with written and oral culturally constructed texts
- Notices and predicts the patterns of regular routines and the passing of time
- Begins to make connections between, and see patterns in the feelings, ideas, words and actions and those of others

Strengthening and developing early writing

☐ What writing behaviours do your children demonstrate?

☐ Where do they need to go next?

☐ What do you need to focus on in your responses to children's early writing?

☐ How will this focus be implemented in your planned activities?

☐ Think about each child's early writing development. How would you describe your 'least' and 'most' capable writer?

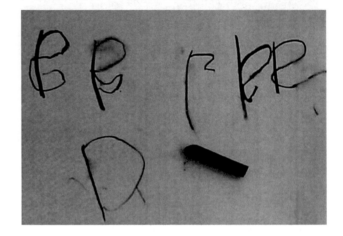

Notes

_____

_____

_____

_____

_____

_____

_____

_____

_____

_____

_____

_____

_____

_____

_____

_____

_____

_____

_____

References & further reading

Bayley R. & Featherstone S. 2010, *Child-initiated Learning*, Featherstone/A&C Black

Bilton, H. 2014, *Playing Outside: Activities, ideas and inspiration for the early year*, (2nd edn) Routledge

Bruce, T. 2004, *Developing Learning in Early Childhood*, Sage Publications

Bruce, T. 2011, *Learning Through Play: For Babies, Toddlers and Young Children*, Hodder Education

Campbell, H. 2002, *The Little Book of Writing*. Featherstone/A&C Black

Clarke, J. & Featherstone, S. 2008, *Young Boys and Their Writing*, Featherstone/A&C Black

Clere, L. 2004, *The Little Book of Bags, Boxes and Trays*, Featherstone/A&C Black

DEEWR 2009, *Early Years Learning Framework*, Commonwealth of Australia

Fox, M. & Mullins, P. 1996, *Hattie and the Fox*, Scholastic

Hall, N. (ed.) 1989, *Writing with Reason*, Hodder Arnold H&S

Hall, N. & Robinson, A. 1995, *Looking at Literacy*, David Fulton Publishers

McKenzie, N. & Scull, J. 2017, *Teaching Children to Write: birth – 8 yrs*, Routledge

Palmer, S., Bayley, R. & Raban, B. 2014, *Foundations of Early Literacy*, Teaching Solutions

Rinaldi, C. 2006, *In Dialogue with Reggio Emilia*, Psychology Press

Roberts, A. 2002, *The Little Book of Props for Writing*, Featherstone/A&C Black

Scull, J. & Raban, B. 2016, *Growing Up Literate: Australian literacy research for practice*, Eleanor Curtain Publishing

Schickedanz, R.A. & Casbergue, R.M. 2009, *Writing in Preschool: Learning to orchestrate meaning and marks* (2nd edn), International Reading Association

You may also be interested in ...

Foundations of Early Literacy

A balanced approach to language, listening and literacy skills in the early years

A comprehensive work outlining the seven key strands of practice for 3- to 6-year-old children, designed to develop the skills, concepts and knowledge underpinning literacy in the early years.